T0147484

OKAY, I'M BETTER NOW!

by

William E. "Tony" Franklin Jr

iUniverse, Inc.
New York   Bloomington

iUniverse books may be ordered through booksellers or by contacting:

*iUniverse
1663 Liberty Drive
Bloomington, IN 47403
www.iuniverse.com
1-800-Authors (1-800-288-4677)*

*Because of the dynamic nature of the Internet, any Web addresses or
links contained in this book may have changed since publication and
may no longer be valid. The views expressed in this work are solely those
of the author and do not necessarily reflect the views of the publisher,
and the publisher hereby disclaims any responsibility for them.*

*ISBN: 978-1-4401-2799-1 (sc)
ISBN: 978-1-4401-2800-4 (ebook)*

Printed in the United States of America

iUniverse rev. date: 3/05/2009

ACKOWLEDGEMENTS

Ellen Franklin Taylor "Auntie" (A1), my mother, my aunt, my father, my life giver all in one person. Without her I wouldn't be here, I'd still have all the feeling on the left side of my body, but I wouldn't be here. I love you most

Vivian Grimes, my birth mother. Thanks for becoming my best friend. I love you always

Naomi for being very important to me and the mother of my children. Love you. Tanya for always being there for me. Love you

Rico, Billy, Fats and Tre; my sons. I ain't giving none of you a dime off of this. I love you all very much most of the time. I'm lucky to be able to have four great sons.

All my sisters and brothers, aunts uncles and cousins who helped mold me into who I am.

My best friend Herb (who made me take the funniest chapter out of the book because it was about him) Myron, for telling me you had kickball practice, Phil, Steve, Rudy, Jerome, Cyrus, Dionne, Kim, Nat, Linda, Carla, and the rest of the family love you all!

Joe Kennedy and Gordon Alston my friends for over 30 years. Thanks for the help with the book. You both proved that you never lose that juvenile ignorance!

To MY ANGEL! The one that got away. You're missed and loved. You will forever hold a very special place in my heart

4word

By Joe Munsta

There's a simple philosophy among the gifted comedians - every good joke must have the hint of true. It is what makes us laugh and what makes us shift uncomfortably in our seats simultaneously. But when you first read the "Tirades", you believe you are reading some ignorant, unimaginable shit. Twisted words formed from a twisted mind induced by a fucked up childhood – or just some real good herb.

So you weren't loved enough – well, fuck you Tony.

But then, you'd be missing the point – wouldn't you?

Like the poets of the Harlem Renaissance who painted an untainted portrait of Black life, Tony Franklin (William Edgar to me) belongs

to a generation of New Rage Comedians –
poets, writers and artists with something to
say. Sometimes profane, okay most of the
time profane, but always provocative-scathing
in nature. Their arsenal – their minds. Their
weapon – the Bloggesphere.

Tony doesn't want you comfortable. He wants
that hint of true to fuck with you. He wants you
to experience a raw, authentic place. A place
where love is a smack upside the head and a
foot in the ass is a lesson to pass down – even if
the foot in the ass comes from a "faggot."

For those of us who grew up in that place,
we are transported through Tony's Tirades.
Transported to where Grandma had holes in
her shoes so her corns could breathe and our
mommas wore horse wigs to church sold by
a big Black woman named Mae. Where "titty
bump" was rap and an Afro moved on your
head like it had a life of its own.

Freddy's dead. Shaft shot his ass because he
was fucking Foxy Brown. That's what I said…

The compilation of tirades in this book
is incidents in his life (our lives, hmm?) that
turned him into the ignorant sum'bitch he is

today. How many of us are afraid of clowns? Well, I was afraid of those painted nightmares too – or as Tony calls them, "those Spawns of Satan." He transforms the "safe, magical place" of the circus into what it really is for children – a place needing a fuckin' exorcism. Clowns "brutally beating each other with those huge bats", while his little brother nibbled on elephant shit. That's sick.

Watch out Tony, Ringling Brothers wants your ass in jail. You can share the cell with Bozo and Ronald McDonald…and that perverted bastard Pee Wee Herman.

Tony snitches the secrets of us forty-something year old men – wet farts and dry dreams, our need to keep the downstairs rug lint free (no gray dick hairs), and the inescapable DUNLAP - "that's where your stomach done lapped over your belt." No one is safe from his warped, straight; dark, crystal-clear wit…not even the boy's momma. That's cold dawg.

I don't know whose idea it was to take Tony from the Bloggesphere and give him a cover and glued pages like Langston Hughes. But, I'm glad they did. Enjoy these Tirades. They are the

William E. "Tony" Franklin Jr

reflections of a rich life of a richer man – my favorite comedian, my friend - Tony Franklin.

CHAPTER 1:

WHY CLOWNS SCARE ME

I saw this kid downtown today that was so afraid of a bird that he almost went into shock. I started to think that if he doesn't get help while young that fear could affect him for the rest of his life like my one fear has. Everyone all ready knows I have a fear of clowns but I never explained why. I blame my mama. She coulda nipped it in the bud which might've allowed me to have a halfway normal childhood . So today I have;

A MESSAGE TO ALL PARENTS.

You have a responsibility to protect your children. Especially during their formative years. You shouldn't disregard the child's dislikes and fears, no matter how minute or juvenile they may seem to you, because sometimes the dislikes and fears that we had as kids can manifest themselves into severe phobias as adults. They can overwhelm and consume our day to day existence and be a detriment to our very way of life. I know this because I am a victim of my parents lack of action in helping me overcome the effects that one horrific moment in my childhood has placed upon me.

Here's my story;

Mama took me to my first circus at the age of 4. I remember the anticipatory joy flowing thru my body as we waited in line at the Washington Coliseum. The thoughts of the elephants, tigers, acrobats and cotton candy had my little heart racing with excitement. I was even happier when we got to our seats; FRONT ROW CENTER RING! So close I could almost reach out and touch the performers. LIFE WAS GREAT! NO child could've been happier than I on that day.

Then, the moment that changed my life occurred. A moment etched in my brain; a moment that has adversely affected my life in a way that still remains. THE CLOWNS CAME OUT!!! They began riding their waayy too little bikes, brutally beating each other with those HUGE BATS (yet never bruising or bleeding!), and using what I still believe to this day was "THE DEVILS WORK", turning ordinary balloons into all kinds of shit! They made balloon dogs, cats, birds, and bears (all which looked alive! evil was in full effect). Then those Spawns of Satan started going around to the front rows collecting children for what I knew was gonna be some kind of Ritual Sacrifice. They're getting close to me so I grab my mama by the arm, look up at her with my best "Pitiful 4 Year Old Baby" face and say "Mommy, I Love You". She looks back at me with a smile and says "I Love You Too Baby". So I'm now thinking she's gonna protect me BUT as soon as Hells Helpers got by us; She voluntarily gave me up to them! I'm now trying to clutch onto her leg and she's got this wicked smile on her face as she says "go on up there with them baby. they won't hurt you". All the adults and remaining kids are cheering as my fingernails bleed from scraping the concrete floor while being dragged to the center of Ring 3. I finally come to grips with my fate and start praying. I get pissed because I don't know a prayer to get me out of this situation. I only know of two prayers because

ALL MAMA EVER TAUGHT ME WAS "NOW I LAY ME DOWN TO SLEEP" AND " GOD IS GREAT AND GOD IS GOOD AND WE THANK HIM FOR OUR FOOD" . SO I

START RECITING THESE TWO PRAYERS OVER AND OVER AND I'M LOOKING OUT AT THE CROWD AND I CAN'T FIND MY MAMA! MMAAAMMAAAA! I YELL WHY YOU LEAVE ME MAAMAA! I DON'T PEE THE BED NO MORE, THAT'S CHUCKIE (MY BABY BROTHER WHO'S SOMEWHERE IN THE AUDIENCE WITH MY TRAITOR ASS MAMA. I KNEW SHE LIKED HIM MORE. IF I MAKE IT OUT OF THIS IMA BASH CHUCKIE'S SKULL IN WITH HIS POTTY TRAINING TOILET. MIGHT AS WELL LET IT GET SOME KIND OF USE). THEN THAT LITTLE 6 INCH CAR PULLS UP AND ABOUT 200 MORE CLOWNS GET OUT. I SCREAM, "THATS THE DEVILS WORK! BACK YOU SATANIC BASTARDS! BACK! I REBUKE YOU IN THE NAME OF JESUS!" SO THEY'RE CIRCLE US KIDS AND I START PRAYING AGAIN, "GOD IS GREAT....." AND I COULD'VE SWORN I HEARD THE DAMN CLOWNS SAYING THE SAME PRAYER! I KNOW THEY'RE GOING TO EAT US! SO I ACCEPT MY FATE AND PASS OUT ONLY TO BE AWAKENED BY MY SELL OUT ASS MAMA SAYING "WAKE UP BABY. THAT MUST'VE BEEN TOO MUCH EXCITEMENT FOR YOU. I'M TAKING YOU HOME" I

WRAP MY ARMS AROUND HER NECK AND SHE'S CARRYING ME TO THE CAR. WE GET TO THE CAR AND IT'S 6 INCHES TALL. I SIMULTANEOUSLY SCREAM, PISS MY PANTS AND CRY. I LOOK UP AT HER TO SAY "MAMA WHY?" AND SHE'S GOT THIS BRIGHT RED NOSE AND WHITE ASS MOUTH AND CHUCKIE'S GOT THIS BIG BLUE MOUTH; SO I PASS OUT AGAIN. I WAKE UP AT HOME IN MY BED BUT FOREVER TORMENTED BY THEM DAMN CLOWNS!

I realized about 20 years later during intense psycho-therapy that my mama wasn't a clown, she just had too much to drink so her nose changed colors and her mouth was just ashy and CHUCKIE ate all his and my cotton candy so that's why his mouth was blue (that punk was sick for a week because I dropped my cotton candy in elephant shit while being sold to the clowns and he thought the shit crumbs was chocolate sprinkles). But if mama had've gotten me help back then I would not have this fear today, so THANKS FOR FUCKIN ME UP MAMA!

okay, I'm better now!

CHAPTER 2:

WHY I WHIP MY KIDS ASSES

While watching the heartbreaking story on the news about the 16 year old who during an argument, stabbed and fatally wounded his own father I began to think just how we as a society and the government are letting this generation of children down. I can remember in the early 80's when then downfall began. With parents being arrested for beating their kids to teacher's being fired for corporal punishment (which in my day was the norm), Uncle Sam is making our offspring undisciplined, unmannerly burdens on society. Growing up I would've never had the nerve to pick up my mama's phone to call social services if she hit me because I know that if they came to her house; she'd either let them take me or make me wanna leave if they left me there. The point I'm trying to convey is that whippin your kids ass ain't gonna kill them. If the ass kickins I took didn't kill me I know the shit parents would do today would cause little irreparable damage to the bodies or minds of these fucked up kids today. I honestly believe that my mama (who I believe to this day was part pimp, because of her beatdown methods. she perfected the "C&P ASS WHIPPIN". what's that you ask? that's when you make someone hold the yellow pages phonebook against their ribs and you take your fist or in my mamas case; a baseball bat and hit the book as hard as you can, causing the holder severe pain and sometimes internal bleeding while not leaving any visible bruises) made me the somewhat law abiding person i am today and if she hadn't whipped my ass I'd be more fucked up than I actually am. What we need today is someone to fuck these little future convicts and streetwalkers asses up like my Mama did me and my siblings.

Now that I think about it;

MY MAMA'S CRAZY ASS SHOULDA BEEN IN JAIL. FOR CHILD ABUSE, MALICIOUS WOUNDING, ATTEMPTED MURDER, AND DESTROYING GOVERNMENT PROPERTY! I LOVE MY MOM BUT CHARGES SHOULD BE FILED. THEY NEED TO GO TO THE CEMETERY, DIG HER ASS UP, HANDCUFF HER DEMENTED ASS (THEY CAN USE THE

ONES SHE USED ON US) AND CART HER MOLE AND MAGGOT INFESTED CARCASS TO JAIL! THE BEATINGS SHE PUT ON ME WERE NOT ONLY PHYSICALLY DAMAGING BUT MENTALLY ABUSIVE. THERE WERE SO MANY; LIKE THE "I DON'T KNOW HOW TO USE A BELT SO EVERY TIME I SWING BACK I HIT MYSELF AND GET MADDER SO IMA WHIP YO ASS LONGER" BEATDOWN, TO THE "THROW HIS ASS DOWN TO THE FLOOR BY HIS HAIR AND STEP ON HIS THROAT" MASSACRE. BUT HERE IS MY LIST OF:

TONY'S MAMA'S TOP
5 ASS WHIPPIN TECHNIQUES

5: SHE ONCE PULLED A SEEDLING (ONE OF THOSE BABY TREES WITH THE LITTLE WOODEN FENCE AROUND IT) OUT THE GROUND BY THE ROOT WITH HER BARE HANDS AND BEAT ME WITH IT

4: THE HALF A HULA HOOP ASS WHIPPIN (SELF EXPLANATORY, BUT SHE AIN'T HAVE TO CUT MY HULA HOOP IN HALF LIKE THAT. SHE WAS JUST EVIL)

3: THE WHOLE HOUSE SMACK. SHE COULDN'T FIND ANYTHING TO HIT ME WITH SO SHE PICKED ME UP BY THE THROAT AND REPEATEDLY THREW ME AGAINST THE SIDE OF OUR HOUSE. AND YES IT WAS MADE OF BRICK!

2: THE "AM I MY BROTHER'S BEATER!". MY BROTHER AND I WERE FIGHTING AND MY MOM COULDN'T FIND ANYTHING TO BEAT US WITH SO SHE PICKED MY BROTHER UP BY THE THROAT (SEE A THEME STARTING?) AND PROCEEDED TO WHIP MY ASS WITH MY BROTHER. THEN SHE'D REVERSE THE PROCESS AND BEAT MY BROTHER WITH ME.

AND THE GREATEST AND MOST PSYCHOTIC TECHNIQUE INVENTED BY MY MEDIEVAL MAMA IS

1: THE "STATION WAGON DRAGGIN" I HAD A PAPER ROUTE WHEN I WAS 10 YRS OLD. IT SHOULD'VE TAKEN ME 20 MINUTES TO DELIVER MY 25 PAPERS BUT ONE DAY I WANTED TO PLAY KICKBALL, SO 3 HRS AFTER I LEFT HOME MY WORRIED MOM DROVE

MY ROUTE AND FOUND ME. SHE PROCEEDED TO PUMMEL ME WITH LEFTS AND RIGHT REMINISCENT OF THE GREAT WELTERWEIGHT FIGHTERS OF HER TIME. SHE THEN THREW ME IN THE MIDDLE OF THE STREET W/ THE SHOPPING CART I USED TO CARRY MY PAPERS AND TOLD ME "NIGGA RUN!", I RAN. NOT FAST ENOUGH FOR HER SO SHE GOT BEHIND ME IN HER 1972 STATION WAGON AND EVERY TIME I SLOWED DOWN SHE'D BUMP ME WITH THE CAR SO I'M RUNNING UPHILL WITH A DAMN SHOPPIN CART, TIRED FROM THE WHIPPIN AND THE KICKBALL GAME (WHICH I MUST SAY WAS FUN BECAUSE I WAS 10 YEARS OLD. THATS THE ONLY TIME A MAN SHOULD BE PLAYING KICKBALL MYRON!!!) AND I SLOW DOWN AGAIN. THIS TIME SHE HITS ME AND I FALL UP UNDER THE CAR, SHE RUNS OVER THE TIPS OF MY FINGERS AND DRAGS ME FOR ABOUT 10 FEET. SHE GETS OUT THE CAR STANDS MY ASPHALT RAVAGED BODY UP, LOOKS AROUND FOR THE COPS, SMACKS THE SHIT OUTTA ME

FOR DENTING THE FRONT OF HER CAR (IGNORING THE DAZED LOOK IN MY EYES AND OBVIOUS CONCUSSION) AND SPED UP THE HILL TOWARDS OUR HOUSE WHILE SHOUTING "YOU BETTER BEAT ME HOME NIGGA!" SO I'M LIMPING AS FAST AS I CAN WITH MULTIPLE FRACTURES, A CONTUSION THE SALT FROM MY SWEAT PIERCING THE OPEN WOUNDS AND ALL THE SKIN FROM MY LEFT SIDE STUCK TO THE PAVEMENT OF 21ST & MARYLAND AVE NE. I MAKE IT HOME (AFTER HER) AND SHE'S STANDING IN FRONT OF THE HOUSE WITH THE NEIGHBORS LAUGHING THEIR ASSES OFF. MAMA YOU WERE FUCKED UP!

My point is this; beatings like that are needed today more than they were when my generation was growing up, so Mama wherever you are; I Love You for damn near killing me so that I can be alive today.

okay, I'm better now

CHAPTER 3:

WHY I'M NOT MARRIED

Today is a bitter sweet day for me. it is the anniversary of my last divorce and it's gotten me feeling somewhat nostalgic. as i sit here remembering the good time (there was only one, hence the non pluralization) that i shared with the person i truly believed was gonna be my cell.. i mean soul mate, and i say to myself; "Self", WHY THE FUCK DIDN'T YOU LEAVE THAT FUCKIN COW 20 YEARS AGO INSTEAD OF 12 , shit I left better bitches than this. The bitch I left b4 I left this bitch is the reason why I ended up with this bitch(even though i didn't know her retarded as 20 years ago, i shoulda left the bitch i had before her just for being fucked up and making me leave her; which led to me being with psycho chunk). THE MAIN REASONS WE SPLIT WERE THAT SHE WAS #1: DUMB AS A BAG OF ROCKS AND 2:"HAPPY FAT" let me explain;

How Dumb was she? read on;

My Brother and I decided we'd have a "who's wife the stupidest contest", so we called them both while they were out shopping to pick up a few items for us. we asked them to get us a left handed hammer and a can of plaid paint. my brothers wife immediately told him "WHAT THE FUCK DO YOU TAKE ME FOR NIGGA? DO I LOOK STUPID TO YOU? (GLAD SHE DIDN'T ASK ME THAT) I'LL BUST YOU IN YO MUTHA FUCKIN HEAD WITH A HAMMER. AND I'LL USE MY LEFT HAND" to which my brother replied; "DO IT!" when he came out of the coma a few weeks later he asked me "what did your wife do" to which i replied; "THAT DUMB ASS SEA DONKEY IS STILL OUT LOOKIN FOR THE HAMMER AND PAINT! I WIN! MY WIFE'S DUMMER THAN YOUR WIFE (sung to the tune of the old ken-l-ration dog food commercial) MY WIFES DUMMER THAN.......then I began to think, Hey; That bitch is really dumb!"

Now i know most of the women are saying "i bet you didn't call her names when you were sleeping with her" and I say to you; you're right!

I COULDN'T SLEEP WITH HER FREIGHT TRAIN MIMICKING SNORIN ASS. I AIN'T GET NO REST FOR 3 YEARS. I HAD BAGS UNDER MY EYES THAT LOOKED EXACTLY LIKE HER FAT ASS MAMAS TITTIES. AND BROTHAS THE OLD SAYING IS TRUE, LOOK AT THE MAMA BECAUSE THAT'S WHAT YOU'RE GONNA BE DATING IN 10 YEARS.

Now i guess the women will say "you know what i mean, when she was giving you the pussy, she wasn't a bitch", and i say to you;

YES THE FUCK SHE WAS! I LIKE ALL MEN JUST DON'T CARE ABOUT HOW BITCHY SHE WAS FOR THAT 10 MINUTE PERIOD. AND SHE WAS COMPLETLY BITCHY.

How Fat was she? read on

Now while she was pregnant with our son she gain a few dozen pounds and I still found her attractive and loved her dearly. i encouraged and supported her in every way. *she was carrying my child* .

After our son was born she gained another few dozen DOZEN pounds (that 12 lbs x 12), so trying to stay supportive, i got us a gym membership but NO she was too self conscious to go out so i bought her Tae Bo tapes and strategically placed them in her high traffic area ; the refrigerator the bathroom and next to the TV . well after a month of nonuse and rapid weight gain I get to my front door and hear a commotion. as i fix me ears to the sound coming from in the house i get excited. IT'S THE BILLY BLANKS TAPE!! SO I FUMBLE W/MY KEY TRYING TO OPEN THE DOOR AND I'M SO HAPPY MY HANDS ARE TREMBLING. I UNLOCK THE DOOR AND I'M ABOUT TO COMMEND HER FOR TAKING THIS MAJOR STEP AND THIS FUCKIN HEFFER IS SITTING ON THE COUCH WITH A BOX OF ICE CREAM A BAG OF COOKIES AND THE REMOTE WATCHIN THIS TAPE LIKE A FUCKIN MOVIE! SHE TELLS ME IN BETWEEN CHEWS BELCHES AND FARTS "I'M TIRED FROM WATCHIN THIS AND I GOT HUNGRY"

I WANTED TO FORCE FEED THIS HAM SHANK CRISCO UNTIL HER FAT ASS ARTERIES BURST!

That's why I believe that a marriage license should be like a drivers license; after 4 yrs if you don't want it you just don't renew it! I HATE HER!!!!!!!!!!!

okay, I'm better now

CHAPTER 4:

WHY I HATE OLD CARS

Again I had my tirade for this chapter ready and then something else pissed me off to the point that i must speak on it now or run the risk of stabbing somebody in the throat with a pencil (not a sharp pointed pencil; but one that I've drawn 10 million o's with until the tip is nice and round, so that a "puncture occurs instead of an actual stab)

I understand that with the astounding cost of gas people must do anything they can to save on fuel. My first suggestion would be take public transportation or even walk but i understand that these aren't viable options for some, although it should be for a few STUPID BASTARDS that actually have vehicles. here's a story about one such person; while out on a 3am food run recently, we noticed a 24 hr McDonalds . now at this time of morning the only option is drive thru; so we pull up the driveway to the drive thru and behind this IGNORANT BASTARD driving a 1981 primer gray convertible geo storm (with the red datsun door and green ford hood). I see this car and immediately tell the driver to back up but by then another car has pulled behind us so now we're trapped. there were 2 cars in front of the geo so this SONUVABITCH has to cuts his car off so that the people in front could actual hear and order (and to save gas and possibly lives because the oil had that PIECE OF SHIT SMOKIN LIKE HE WAS SELLIN BAR B Q OUTTA THE ENGINE, THE CONVERTIBLE TOP WAS ALL RIPPED UP AND IT WAS WINDY SO IT LOOKED LIKE THAT MUTHA FUCKA WAS WAVING AT ME; HE HAD A PAIR NASTY ASS DRAWS WHERE THE GAS CAP OUGHTA BE AND THIS BACKWOODS TOBACCO CHEWIN NO SHOES WEARING IN LUV WITH HIS SISTER ASS COUNTRY NIGGA HAD THE NERVE TO HAVE A PIECE OF CARDBOARD STAPLED TO THE BACK WINDOW THAT SAID "STOLEN TAGS". AIN'T NOBODY STOLE SHIT OFF THAT RAGGEDLY MUTHA FUCKA UNLESS THEY STOLE IT BACK FROM HIS ASS!!!) and it cuts off. Now he gets out and pops the hood and looks around like "this shit ain't never happened before", goes to the hood, comes back to us, knocks on the window and says "Yo, My Man; do you have any jumper cables?" I tell him; "MUTHA FUCKA , YOU THE ONE WITH THE RAGGEDLY ASS RIDE; WHY THE FUCK DON'T YOU HAVE NO JUMPER CABLES! WHY DON'T YOU PUSH THAT SHIT OUT OF THE DRIVE THRU SO WE CAN GET OUR FOOD NIGGA! OR BETTER YET, USE THOSE FLINTSTONE FEET YOUR WOMAN GOT AND HAVE HER PEDDLE THAT PREHISTORIC PIECE OF SHIT OUTTA THE DRIVE THRU YOU DROOPY EYED SONUVABITCH!" (DID I MENTION HE WAS ABOUT 80 YRS OLD. WE KNOW FROM PAST TIRADES THAT I CAN'T FIGHT SO IF I'MA TALK SHIT TO SOMEONE I KNOW I CAN TAKE EM OUT). SO HE TURNS HIS WALKER AROUND AND GOES BACK TO THE CAR, MAKES HIS OLD ASS WOMAN GET OUT (SHE WAS ABOUT 90 AND ALL YOU COULD SEE WAS HER BREATH PRINTS ON THE PASSENGER SIDE WINDOW. OLD BITCH WAS JUST HAPPY TO BE ALIVE) AND PUSH WHILE HE STEERS. NOW SHE'S HITTIN THE FRONT OF OUR CAR WITH THAT BIG ASS

OXYGEN TANK ON HER BACK AS SHE ALTERNATES BETWEEN WHEEZES AND PUSHES, SO AFTER ABOUT 15 MINUTES SHE'S FINALLY GOT THE CAR OUT SO WE CAN GET OUR FOOD.

NOW THE STUPID ASS CLERK DONE FUCKED UP OUR ORDER SO I ASK THIS IDIOT "HOW HARD IS IT TO FUCK UP MCNUGGETS AND FRIES?" SHE GOT 2 CHEESEBURGERS AND AN OLD ASS SALAD IN THE BAG WITH 200 PACKS OF MCNUGGET SAUCE BUT NO NUGGETS! SHE SAYS "I THOUGHT THAT'S WHAT YOU ORDERED" THE BILL WAS $32.16 (2 BURGERS AND A SALAD FOR $32) I GAVE THIS BITCH $40.16; IT TOOK HER ANOTHER 15MINUTES TO FIGURE THE CHANGE. WE FINALLY GET OUTTA THERE AFTER AN HOUR; POPS AND HIS RIB STAND DONE GOT A JUMP AND HE'S GONE; SO WE PULL OFF AND GO 1 BLOCK AND AT THE LIGHT THIS BASTARD DONE CUT HIS CAR OFF TO SAVE GAS AND IT WON'T START AGAIN. THIS TIME THE TANK CARRYING BITCH IS WHEEZIN HER ASS TO THE CAR AND ALL I CAN THINK WHEN MUTHA FUCKAS GET TOO

OLD TO BE ACTUALLY PRODUCTIVE; THEY SHOULD BE TAKEN TO THE SAME CLINIC AS THAT BAD ASS 7 YR OLD (*SEE PREVIOUS TIRADE) AND PUT TO SLEEP.

SO I THINK NIGGAS IN FUCKED UP CARS AND OLD PEOPLE SHOULD DIE!

okay, I'm better now

CHAPTER 5:

WHY SOME PEOPLE NEED TO BE IN JAIL

Today I had jury duty and I feel good about doing my civic duty and being part of the judicial process.

Okay i'm lying my ass off. this is the most annoying thing that has ever happened to me. WHY THE FUCK DO I HAVE TO BE FORCED TO TAKE A WORK DAY AND SPEND IT AROUND THE DREADS OF SOCIETY FOR 40 FUCKIN DOLLARS! I did everything humanly possible to Not get picked for a trial because i know i couldn't be impartial. ALL THOSE BASTARDS WERE GUILTY! so whenever they asked a question such as do you know anyone involved in this case, have you ever been a victim, do you have any weed on you, etc; I raised my hand. It works most of the time, except today. so i'm stuck on a fuckin case tomorrow (we know what my verdict will be. if this bastard didn't do this crime; he's done something or will do something that he should be locked up for. i'm just gonna save some taxpayers money).

So after being dismissed for the day i decided i'd get some enjoyment so i went looking for a case to sit in on. the courts are like a big ass movie theater where you can walk into each room and preview which show you wanna watch for free, so after i found one that looked interesting, i got me a soda and some chips (why don't they sell popcorn @ the courts?)and took a seat to see the show. i have just one question;

Is it just me or does it seemed like the DUMBEST MUTHA FUCKAS ON EARTH are part of this system;

THESE TWO DUMB SONUVABITCHES WERE ON TRIAL FOR BANK ROBBERY, YET THESE SPECIAL ED ASS' GOT NO MONEY AND HAD NO GUN. HERES WHAT THESE FOOLS DID; ONE GUY WORKED AS A TELLER. AND HAD ONE OF HIS BUDDIES HELP HIM. THE PLAN WAS SIMPLE, EXCEPT HE PICKED THE MOST IDIOTIC BASTARD TO HELP HIM.(CRIME TIP: IF

YOU'RE LOOKING FOR AN ACCOMPLICE, NEVER PICK THE FRIEND WHO WAS SO STUPID HE SPENT 5 YRS IN 6TH GRADE)

HIS FRIEND WAS TO COME INTO THE BANK, GO UP TO HIS WINDOW, HAND HIM A NOTE SAYING THIS IS A STICKUP, HE'D GIVE HIM THE MONEY AND THEY'D MEET UP LATER ON AND SPLIT IT UP. GREAT PLAN RIGHT??? WELL THE DAY CAME AND HIS FRIEND COMES INTO THE BANK; HE STANDS IN LINE WITH A STOCKING CAP PULLED DOWN OVER HIS RETARDED ASS FACE! HE ALLOWS PEOPLE TO GO IN FRONT OF HIM UNTIL HIS BUDDIES LINE OPENS UP; THIS IGNORANT BASTARD THEN HANDS HIS BOY A NOTE THAT SAYS, AND I QUOTE;

"DEAR TIM, I GOT A GUN. THIS IS A STICKUP. PUT THE MUNY IN THIS BAG AND NO WUN WILL GIT HURT,

JOE,

P.S. MEET YOU AT YOUR HOUSE TONITE

It took the jury 30 seconds to convict. they didn't even go into the jury room. as soon as

27

the case ended they just told the judge their verdict. So I stood up and applauded (they don't really like that) & the convicts got upset and yelled "Nigga I'ma Bust YO Ass", to which i replied "no, you'll be getting your ass busted. don't drop the soap big homie" that made me think about prison and my tip is this ;

I've come to the conclusion that with my baby soft skin and boyish good looks, if i went to prison i'd be swept up before the first lights out . so i'll just tell all my friends now that if we ever commit a crime and we running and i get caught; stop running because **WE'RE CAUGHT** !

DON'T DO A CRIME WITH ME

PS, Tomorrow them Niggas still guilty!

okay, I'm better now

CHAPTER 6:

WHY I HATE MY KIDS

As a father of four sons (who all live with me) I am proud that they are growing into great young men. Raising boys to be MEN has been the toughest job I've ever had to do but the rewards of seeing them mature into the respectful gentlemen they are becoming is priceless. It hasn't always been easy. There were times when I really had 2nd thoughts about them being here. it led me to ask;

Is all this aggravation for a grand total of 9 1/2 minutes of pleasure really worth it. I should've left them bastards in a condom. they get on my nerves so bad at times, here's one of them

My sons know that if a joke is funny and I can use it in my act and nobody dies then no one gets in trouble SO when my middle kids were 9&12 they shared a bedroom. my 9 yr old would get up every morning at the crack of dawn and take a shit. so my 12 yr old decided to super glue the rim and seat of his drawers so in the a.m. my 9yr old tries to take his dump & can't get his draws off. he shits on his self so he hits his brother (who's laughing like he dropped acid) in the head w/ a miniature baseball bat & splits his head open. So i come in their room to see a shitty kid crying and stinkin like a mutha fucka and a bloody maniacal laughing kid who's slowly losing consciousness but still crakin the fuck up. i get them to the hospital and the law and social services are questioning me like i'm a fuckin perve (i think the cops were from SVU). after i finally convince them of what really happened they let me go check on these bastards. so i'm sittin in the hospital and i begin to think;

I HAVE ALWAYS BEEN ANTI ABORTION (BUT PRO CHOICE). BUT IF YOU'RE GONNA ALLOW IT RAISE THE AGE LIMIT. WOMAN CAN HAVE IT UP TO THEIR 2ND TRIMESTER. HELL NO! IT SHOULD BE LEGAL UNTIL THE CHILD IS ABOUT 7 YEARS OLD. BY THEN YOU GOT A GOOD IDEA ABOUT WHAT TYPE OF PERSON THAT LITTLE BASTARD IS GONNA BE!

IF HE/SHE IS FUCKED UP YOU CAN JUST DROP THAT MUTHA FUCKA OFF AT THE CLINIC! CAN YOU IMAGINE HOW GOOD A PARENTING WEAPON THAT'D BE? I KNOW FOR A FACT THAT I PROBABLY WOULDN'T HAVE NO KIDS IF THAT WAS LAW. HELL; I WOULDN'T HAVE ANY FRIENDS EITHER BECAUSE I'M SURE OUR PARENTS WOULDA PUT OUR ASSES TO SLEEP.

after that I really couldn't stand those shittin eatin "pussy stretchin so it ain't no more fun" ass little rat bastards!!!!!! my job after that was to make them miserable as I am

I EVEN gave them nicknames that coincided with events that transpired the nights they were conceived. they're as follows:

1st son: Ronrico-after the cheap rum I drank that led to me boning his ugly ass mama

2nd son: Broken Rubber- self explanatory (still bonin ugly ass mama)

3rd son: "OOPs" mama said she was fixed (AGAIN! SAME Ugly ass mama)

4th son: "Shoulda Got Head" (his mama is ugly too!)

HERE'S MY TIP; KILL YOUR KIDS BEFORE THEY KILL YOU!!!!!

okay, I'm better now

CHAPTER 7:

WHY I HATE GETTING OLD

like most men; when the onset of middle age hit I didn't take it well. i was confronted with the mysterious pains in the knees and back that so often accompany reaching the age of 40. certain aspects that i took for granted were now backwards. (backwards you ask??? like now i have wet farts and dry dreams instead of the other way around.)

Most alarming are the changes to my physical appearance. I now have to work HARD to not have the "DUNLAP" (DUNLAP you ask??? that's where your stomach done lapped over your belt; (giving the appearance of a hide-a-dick), BUT nothing says old more than gray hair. now many people will say gray makes black men look distinguished. to me it says "old and somebody worrying the shit outta you"

I began dyeing my hair a few years ago, so i learned which ones to use, how long they last etc . There are only a few things i need to know. for one;

WHY THE FUCK DON'T THEY SAY ON THE BOX THAT THE DYE IS ONLY FOR USE ON THE UPPER HEAD!!

I WAS IN THE SHOWER AND NOTICED THAT MY "LOWER REGION" HAD BECOME ALMOST ENTIRELY GRAY; SO I FIGURED SINCE THE BOX SAID "NO LYE" , "NON ALERGETIC" & MOST IMPORTANTLY "NO BURNING"; IT WAS COOL. FUCK NO, AFTER ABOUT 30 SECONDS MY NUTS STARTED STEAMING, SMOKE WAS PROTRUDING FROM ABOVE MY DICK, ALL I COULD SAY WAS "WHOOOO" AS I WAVED MY HAND OVER MY SHIT LIKE ALI AT THE OLYMPICS . THEN THE HAIRS BEGAN TO FALL INTO THE TUB LIKE THE TWIN TOWERS AFTER THE PLANES HIT; REVEALING A REDDISH GREEN RASH WHOS COLORS WERE MORE VIVID THAN ANY RAINBOW I'D EVER SEEN(I SEEM TO REMEMBER SAYING "OOOH LOOK ATDA PWETTY COLAAS"). RIGHT BEFORE I PASSED OUT I LOOKED AT THE HAIRS

LAYING IN MY TUB AND NOTICED THEY WERE STILL GRAY!!! AFTER ALL THIS SHIT THEY WERE STILL FUCKIN GRAY!!! I WAS TAKEN TO THE HOSPITAL (AND I MUST SAY THAT PARAMEDICS AREN'T REAL SYMPATHETIC TO BROTHAS IN THIS SITUATION) WHERE I WAS RIDICULED, THEN RASH OINTMENTED, DIAPERED AND SENT HOME TO AWAIT THE EVEN MORE UNCOMFORTABLE "REGROWTH". (ALL THIS COULD'VE BEEN AVOIDED IF WE HAD A DICK ISLE W/ NUT GRAY-BE-GONE "REALLY NO BURN" PUBE COLOR AND RELAXER)

JUST THINKING ABOUT THIS STILL PAINS ME!!!

okay, I'm better now

CHAPTER 8:

WHY I BELIEVE MEN ARE DISCRIMINATED AGAINST

I believe that we live in a country that promotes divisiveness between the races, the classes, but most of all, the sexes. Some things are blatantly open and others are done so subtle that we miss it; even if it's right in front of our eyes. One of the Biggest perpetrators of this inequality in our country is the Supermarket/ Drug Store! These places are completely biased against men. What the hell am I saying you ask??? **WHERE THE FUCK IS THE DICK ISLE???** think about it; you can walk into any Safeway, Giant, CVS, Shoppers, etc and find an isle that is 100% dedicated to women. From the tampon, to the douche; you'll see cascades of feminine products as far as the eye can see. this is okay, My only question is; **WHY AM I LEFT OUT! DID YOU EVER THINK THAT A MAN MIGHT WANT OR**

William E. "Tony" Franklin Jr

DESERVE THE SAME OPPORTUNITY TO SMELL "SPRINGTIME FRESH" AS A WOMAN?? WE HAVE DAYS TOO WHEN WE MIGHT NEED THAT EXTRA HELP KEEPING THE "SALTY POND WATER" SMELL OFF OUR NUTS; WHERE'S MY DDS(DICK DEODARIZER SPRAY)? OKAY I THINK ALL MEN WILL AGREE THAT THE "DOUCHE"; YOU LADIES CAN KEEP FOR YOURSELVES BUT CAN'T WE AT LEAST GET A "CHEESE" REMOVAL SYSTEM IN THE STORES. I CAN SEE THE COMMERCIAL NOW (DURING THE NBA PLAYOFFS WOULD BE THE PERFECT TIME); DENZELL WOULD WALK IN FRONT OF THE CAMERA AND SAY "HEY FELLAS; HAVE YOU EVER BEEN WORKING ALL DAY, IT'S 80 DEGREES, YOU'RE A LITTLE TART BUT YOU WANT TO HIT THE CLUB AFTER WORK BUT YOU DON'T WANT TO GO ALL THE WAY HOME TO CLEAN UP AND CHANGE. WELL GUYS TRY THIS ; THE PORTABLE KIWI STRAWBERRY NUTT WASH! IT'LL KEEP YOUR BALLS TASTY FOR HOURS" TRY OUR OTHER FLAVAS THE LADIES SAVA LIKE MARGARITA (GOES WELL WITH THAT "SALTY" TASTE) OR THE NEWEST

ONE COFFEE CAKE AND DOUGHNUTS (MADE FOR THE BIG GIRL LOVERS)" ALL I ASK FOR IS EQUALITY!

okay, I'm better now

CHAPTER 9:

I JUST WANNA FUCK
WITH MY FRIEND

This is a true story. The names have been changed to protect the ignorant.

I had my topic all picked out for this week; I'd even started writing but on Saturday i received a call from a friend; (we'll call him Herm*) he tells me that he just talked to one of our other friends; (we'll call him MYRON) to ask where he was. to which MYRON* replied, "**at kickball practice**"! Now i commend anyone for joining leagues and playing sports at our age but i have a few questions; **WHAT THE FUCK IS A GROWN ASS MAN DOING IN A KICKBALL LEAGUE?IF YOU WERE 10 YEARS OLD IT'D BE SOMEWHAT ACCEPTABLE BUT AT DAMN NEAR 40 KICKBALL LEAGUE SAYS GAY! FAG! AND IF YOU SAY YOU**

JOINED TO MEET WOMEN KNOW THIS; NO SELF RESPECTING WOMEN WOULD DATE A MAN SHE MET IN A KICKBALL LEAGUE BECAUSE SHE KNOWS HE'S GAY! HELL, A DIKE WOULDN'T JOIN A KICKBALL LEAGUE LET ALONE A REAL MAN! AND WHAT THE HELL DO THEY HAVE TO PRACTICE? HOW STUPID DO YOU HAVE TO BE TO NOT KNOW; ROLL, KICK, RUN! THATS ALL IT IS TO THAT. I'D LOVE TO SEE YOUR UNIFORM. A KICKBALL LEAGUES UNIFORM HAS TO BE SPANDEX AND ONE PIECE WITH THE LITTLE SNAPS UNDER THE CROTCH; BUT DON'T WORRY BECAUSE ANY MAN IN A KICK BALL LEAGUE DON'T HAVE NUTS SO THE BUTTONS DON'T BOTHER YOU ONE BIT! I BET THE LEAGUE SPONSOR IS MASENGIL AND ANAL-EEZE. SUPPOSE YOU GET INJURED; HOW MANLY CAN YOU SAY "I WAS RUNNIN DOWN A POP FLY OFF THE FOOT OF MARCELL "PUSSYFOOT" SYLVESTER (HE'S THE DIVA OF THE LEAGUE. HE GOT HIS NAME BECAUSE HE HAD HIS TOES ON HIS RIGHT FOOT FUSED TOGETHER TO RESEMBLE A VAGINA. HE KICKS BAREFOOT TO

DAMAGED THE COOCHIE. HOW HE HATES IT!) WHEN I FELT MY HIP BREAK" GUESS YOU'RE STILL TRYING TO FIGURE OUT WHY "PUSSYFOOT" WAS THE FIRST ONE THERE TO HELP YOU; WITH HIS RECTAL THERMOMETER AND TRYING TO GIVE YOU MOUTH TO MOUTH. MYRON I'D KICK YOU IN THE BALLS IF YOU HAD BALLS FOR JOININING A KICKBALL LEAGUE!

okay, i'm better now

CHAPTER 10:

WHY I'M SCARED OF HOMOSEXUALS

Now, I believe that ones sexual preference is their own business. people can choose to love whomever they please whether it be opposite or same sex. it is the individuals choice. my only criticism would be that if you're gay; be gay. don't hide it. do not try to make yourself out to be something you're not. there should be a law that gay men must act and dress as gay men (i.e.; call each other girlfriend, speak with a lisp, wear leopard print leotards, etc). and most of all, stay out of men's conversations. case in point; one Monday morning i was on the train to work where a group of guys were talking about the previous days football games. we conversed in a spirited way as real men do when speaking of the rivalries of their favorite teams. so my stop came; i exited the train along with a few other "Football Junkies". three of us are standing on

45

the escalators as they go up when another of our orators walked up the escalator; and as he passed us; grabbed me on the ass!!!!! not an accidental like brush, but a full on "grab both cheeks with one hand while trying to tip the anus with your middle finger" type ass grab. now the men standing have gotten over their initial shock and have broken out in the most maniacal laughter known! the "super bitch" is now standing at the turnstile (where you pay to leave the metro station) with his hand on his hip smiling at me. so, i do what any red blooded man would do; I CRACKED THIS PUNK WITH THE BEST "STRAIGHT" RIGHT HAND I'D EVER THROWN! and he lets out a semi scream/yell that could've come right out of a Prince CD which got my blood pumping so i throw a right hook ;and the screams start even longer and longer and louder! **I HAD NO IDEA SOUNDS LIKE THAT COULD COME FROM ME!!!!!!!!! THIS FAGGOT WAS BEATING THE HOLY SHIT OUT OF ME. NOW I AIN'T NO SLOUCH WHEN IT COMES TO BATTLIN BUT THIS GUMP WAS TOO DAMN GOOD! HE KEPT TRYING TO GET ME ON MY STOMACHE SO I HAD TO DO THE "GIRL FIGHT EYES CLOSED WINDMILL**

WHILE CLINCHIN YOUR ASS CHEEKS SO TIGHT A SEWING NEEDLE COULDN'T ENTER DON'T CRY NIGGA" MOVES. I WAS SO HAPPY WHEN METRO COPS SHOWED UP AND PULLED THIS PUNK OFF ME,; BUT I HAD TO SAVE FACE SO I JUMP UP FIXED MY SHIRT AND HAIR AND THEN PROCLAIMED (WITH A SLIGHT TEAR IN MY EYE) "IF YOU EVER TOUCH ME LIKE THAT, I'LL WHIP YOUR ASS AGAIN PUNK!!!!!!!!" TO WHICH THE COPS REPLY IN UNISON "IF WE HADN'T GOT HERE THAT FAGGOT WOULD STILL BE KICKIN YOUR ASS!" THEN THIS SUPER STRONG TURD BURGLAR LOOKS AT ME AND SAYS SOMETHING THAT WILL HAUNT ME FOR THE REST OF MY LIFE!, HE SAYS "IF YOU EVER TOUCH ME AGAIN, I'LL WHIP YOUR ASS THEN SUCK YOUR DICK!!!!!" NOW TREMBLING WITH FEAR YET TRYING NOT TO SHOW IT; I GET THE MENTAL PICTURE OF ME, LAYING IN THE SUBWAY, BEAT HALF TO DEATH, PANTS DOWN BY MY ANKLES, HUMILIATED YET SOMEWHAT SATISFIED. IN NEED OF A CIGARRETTE! THATS WHY I THINK THERE SHOULD

William E. "Tony" Franklin Jr

BE A LEGAL DRESS CODE FOR FAGGOTS!!!!!!!!!!!!!!!!

okay, i'm better now

CHAPTER 11:

A DAMN DOG

This topics has festered on my mind like a pimple on the inside of a fat woman's thigh for the past year or so; i must get this off my chest. I understand that there are major cultural differences between the peoples; that doesn't mean one race is more advanced or smarter. it just mean we're different. One major difference in white people and every other race (Kim being the exception) is the value they put on their pets. they treat them as if they were family and not just an animal that you have to feed and teach not to shit everywhere and every now and then smack that fucka on the tip of it's nose (okay; they do sound like kids)

I was reading the Local paper and came across the following add;

LOST! 14 year old **BLIND, DIABETIC** brown and white beagle named Lucky.

William E. "Tony" Franklin Jr

$500 reward

Heart wrenching, isn't it? now i only have a few questions

HOW FUCKED UP DO A SITUATION GOTTA BE FOR A BLIND DIABETIC DOG TO RUN AWAY FROM? HOW DID THEY FIND OUT THIS DOG WAS DIABETIC? I CAN UNDERSTAND THAT IT AIN'T HARD TO FIGURE OUT HIS ASS WAS BLIND CUZ HE KEPT RUNNIN INTO SHIT AND YOU KNEW HE WASN'T DRINKIN NO MORE SINCE YOU KICKED YOUR ADDICT ASS BROTHA OUT, BUT THEY TOOK HIS ASS IN AND HAD HIM TESTED FOR DIABETIES. A DOG! I REMEMBER WHEN THEY THOUGHT MY GRANDMA HAD THE SUGA; THEY PUSHED HER ASS DOWN THE STEPS SO SHE COULD BREAK HER HIP AND JUST ASKED THEM TO RUN TESTS WHILE SHE WAS AT THE HOSPITAL. THEN WHEN IT WAS CONFIRMED WE JUST LEFT HER ASS AT THE PARK! IF WE DO THAT TO HUMANS; A DOG AIN'T GOT A CHANCE. AND THEY GAVE THAT DOG THE WRONG NAME CUZ HE SURE DON'T SOUND LUCKY TO ME! HOW DID

HIS BLIND ASS GET OUT THE HOUSE IN THE FIRST PLACE? . IF THEY LOVED HIM SO MUCH WHERE WAS HIS SEEING EYE MAN? WHITE PEOPLE PISS ME OFF. I GOT NEWS FOR YOU; LUCKY CRAWLED HIS DECREPIT OLD (HE'S 98 IN HUMAN YEARS) ASS OUT BACK UNDER THE HOUSE AND WITH THE LAST STRENGTH HE HAD IN HIS BODY DUG HIS GRAVE AND DIED(HE ALL READY HAD A SUIT SINCE YOU BOUGHT HIM ONE 4 HIS 13TH B-DAY)! YA'LL THE ONLY REASON HE BEEN AROUND THIS LONG. HE DIDN'T WANT MEDICAL TREATMENT; HE WANTED TO DIE LIKE A REGULAR DOG. I HOPE THEY FIND HIM SO THEY CAN SPEND THAT 500 ON HIS FUNERAL.

okay, i'm better now

CHAPTER 12:

SOME JOBS JUST AIN'T FOR THEM

I believe that the handicapped whether physical or mental should be given every chance to prosper and grow in their professional lives as well as personal; BUT there are some JOBS that because of their physical limitations these BASTARDS SHOULD NOT BE ALLOWED TO DO! I work at one of the largest law firms in the world (located in downtown DC). they have a large building where each entrance has a security check point with a security officer who checks I D's. with the type of classified information stored here, some that's vital to national security; you'd expect the best of the best providing security; so, **WHY THE FUCK IS THERE A DAMN RETARDED SECURITY GUARD WATCHING THE SIDE OF THE BUILDING THAT I WORK**

ON? THIS FUCKA IS STANDING AT THE CHECKPOINT WITH HIS THICK ASS MR OTIS GLASSES (COMPLETE W/TAPE DOWN THE MIDDLE, SLIGTY COCKED TO THE LEFT SIDE OF HIS FACE DUE TO THE FACT THAT HIS RIGHT EAR IS 4 TIMES THE SIZE OF A NORMAL HUMAN) DROOLIN AND LETTIN ANYBODY THRU BECAUSE HIS RETARDED ASS CAN'T TELL IF THE PICTURE ON THE BADGE IS THE MUTHA FUCKA IN FRONT OF HIM! ALL HE DOES IS SAY "GGA HEA" (THAT SHOULD BE "GO AHEAD" IF SPOKEN IN "NON-TARD"). GOD FORBID SOMETHING HAPPENS AND HE HAS TO CALL FOR BACK-UP. WITH ONLY 2 RELIABLE FINGERS ON EACH HAND HOW THE FUCK IS THIS MONSTER TARD GONNA PUSH THE TALK BUTTON ON THE RADIO? IT TAKES HIM 20 MINUTES TO GET HIS K'NISTCK (THAT'S NIGHT STICK FOR PEOPLE W/ A FULLY FUNCTIONAL BRAIN) OUT THE HOLSTER. HE GOTTA SIT ON THE DAMN FLOOR AND TAKE THAT GOOD FINGER AND POINT THE STICK TO THE GROUND AN DO A SEMI RETARD PUSH UP TO GET THE DAMN THING OUT! YOU DON'T

SEE RETARDED PILOTS OR DRS, SO WHY THE HELL WOULD YOU PUT RAINMAN IN CHARGE OF POSSIBLY SAVING A LIFE. THESE CHEAP BASTARDS HIRED HIM JUST BECAUSE HE WORKS FOR CRAYON AND ALL THE PASTE HE CAN EAT. I WANT A SECURITY GUARD THAT WEARS A WHOLE UNIFORM, NOT THE SHIRT AND PAJAMA PANTS! IS THAT TOO MUCH TO ASK?

okay, I'm better now!

CHAPTER 13:

WHY I HATE THE HOMELESS

This morning I was approached by a homeless man selling a newspaper called "Street Sense" He explained it was a paper written by and for the homeless. first i asked that bastard why the hell he asked me to buy it then. He explained further that he meant "for" them to make some extra money (for drinks and maybe food. definitely not soap)He wasn't pushy in that normal "entertaining homeless guy" way so i was gonna give him a quarter to support his venture; but he tells me the paper is $1.00. so i asked how can your paper be more expensive than the Wash. Post. he told me it had real issues and it was more informative to homeless people AND it had more info than the post.

WHAT THE FUCK KINDA INFORMA-TION DO HOMELESS BASTARDS NEED? WHERE THE WARMEST GRATES ARE IN

THE CITY? TOP 10 DUMPSTERS TO FORAGE IN FOR FOOD?

WHAT THE FUCK!!!!!!!!!!!!!!! I TOLD THIS BASTARD THAT I BET I KNOW SOME INFO YOUR PAPER DON'T HAVE; BET IT DON"T HAVE A EMPLOYMENT SECTION! WHERE THE FUCK IS THE "APARTMENT FOR RENT" SECTION OR EVEN THE ROOM FOR RENT SECTION.

HOW THE HELL CAN YOU CHARGE MORE FOR A NEWSPAPER MADE BY HOMELESS BASTARDS THAN THE WASHINGTON POST? HIS FUCKIN PAPER WAS WRITTEN OVER YESTERDAY'S POST. THEY STOLE WHITE OUT AND COVERED THE WORDS THEN WROTE OVER THEM IN PENCIL!. AFTER YOU READ IT THEY ASK FOR IT BACK, ERASE TODAY'S NEWS AND START ON TOMORROW'S.

okay, I'm all better now

CHAPTER 14:

SOMETIMES I'M JUST SIMPLE

Hello Everyone, I know I'm not the most political person nor do I consider myself an activist; but there are some things that even I feel so strongly about that i feel it's my duty to speak up and out on a topic that causes men so much mental and emotional strain and anguish that something must be done about it. So, I have started an organization to deal with this problem. I will devote my time and money to letting the powers be know **WE WANT A CHANGE DAMMIT!!!!!!!!!!!!**

The organization will be known as M.A.L.A.U or **MEN AGAINST LOW ASS URINALS!!**

I AM SO DAMN SICK OF GOING INTO A PUBLIC RESTROOM AND THE URINAL IS 6 INCHES OFF THE FLOOR AND FILLED WITH JUST ENOUGH WATER TO LEAVE THOSE GOT DAMN PEE FRECKLES ON

THE LEGS OF YOUR PANTS. GOD FORBID YOU'RE WEARING A LIGHT COLORED SUIT THEN EVERYBODY THINKS YOU GOT AN AIMING DEFICIENCY. IT'S FUCKIN UNFAIR!!! WOMAN GOT THE SIT DOWN JOINTS AND THEY CAN PUT A MAN ON THE MOON; WHY OH LORD WHY CAN'T THEY MAKE A URINAL THAT CATERS TO MEN OVER 5 FUCKIN FEET TALL. ENOUGH IS ENOUGH GOT DAMMIT!!!!!!!!

Today while out having lunch I ran into an old acquaintance Sandra Sanders, whom I hadn't seen in over 10 years . She USED to be one of the most beautiful women I'd ever seen in my life; but now it seemed to me that the years had not been kind to her. She had lost a considerable amount of weight and she looked weathered. Me being who I am (and the fact that she dumped me), I had to ask her; "DAMN WHAT THE HELL HAPPENED TO YOU?" She replied that she has been sick for the last 10 years and life has been hard since she can't keep a job because she's in and out of the hospital. I ask her what type of illness and she told me she had Lupus; to which I replied "THANK GOD! I THOUGHT YOU WERE GONNA SAY YOU

HAD THE AIDS!". (See I really didn't care that she was sick, I only cared what kind of sickness she had and if she gave that sickness to me. For a minute there I started feeling ill just thinking that she left a little something in me to remember her by.) Well for some reason she got real upset, called me a Uncaring Rat Bastard and walked off. To which I; being me replied "LOOK FORWARD TO SEEING YOU AGAIN BECAUSE I KNOW THE NEXT TIME I SEE YOU, YOU'LL BE DEAD!" I know that was mean but she dumped me and I never take that well. Then as I was leaving to head back to my office I saw one of my old running Buddies Mike James, who had seemed to drop off the face of the earth a few years back. he too looked as if life had bitch slapped him around so I asked him "NIGGA, WHAT THE HELL HAPPENED TO YOU? YOU BEEN DATING SANDRA SANDERS?" He said "No, I got hooked up with a pretty little thing that had AIDS. She gave it to me and now I'm on my last Days" I said "DAMN!, SUCKS TO BE YOU. I WOULD GIVE YOU A POUND BUT THAT SHIT MIGHT BE IN THE SWEAT ON YOUR HANDS NIGGA. PEACE ! Well I started thinking about the good old days when you could have sex with anybody and the worst thing that happened was you pissed fire, beat the bitches ass who burned you, got a shot in your ass, don't get none for two weeks and start all over again. THEN came herpes, which was STD on steroids. If you got that; you'd beat the bitches ass who gave it to you, invest in a lot of blistex and peroxide for the fever blisters on your lips, use a condom forever (which is what your dumbass should've always been doing), and even though you are now diseased for the rest of your life, you still have the rest of your life! Now the scariest thing ever invented by man has wrecked the "Hookin Up" age. The AIDS Virus has come along and messed life up for everybody! No longer can you meet somebody at the club, fill them full of cheap liquor then take them back home and dent your headboard with their temple WITHOUT thinking of the long term consequences. AIDS has made Herpes the Disease of choice. I bet Mike would give his right arm (if it hasn't fallen off yet) to be diagnosed with Herpes instead of AIDS. So I'm walking back to my office with my headphones on; listening to the OLD SCHOOL JAM "MUST BE THE MUSIC" but I'm thinking about Mike and Sandra and the words to the song begin to change from "I'M JUST A DJ BABY MIXIN FOR YOU. I WILL

NOT STOP UNTIL THIS CLUB NITE IS THRU; MUST BE THE MUSIC" to "I'M JUST A VICTIM OF A DISEASE SO TRUE. CAN'T GET NO PUSSSY CUZ MY BALLS HAVE TURNED BLUE; MUST BE THE HERPES" So I get back to the office and this tune is beatin me in the head and I knew unless I finished it AND shared it, I'd get no work done, so here it is MUST BE THE HERPES Sung to the tune of "Must Be The Music" FLASHIN PAINS, UP AND DOWN MY BALLS, MAN THE HERPES WILL HAVE U DRIVIN THE WALLS I'M JUST A VICTIM OF A DISEASE SO TRUE, CAN'T GET NO PUSSY CUZ MY BALLS HAVE TURNED BLUE chorus MUST BE THE HERPES (MUST BE THE HERPES) THAT'S BURNIN MY DICK; MUST BE THE HERPES (MUST BE THE HERPES) THAT MAKES MY BALLS ITCH MUST BE THE HERPEEES; NOW BABY THATS BURNIN MY DICK; MUST BE THE HERPES; THAT MAKES MY BALLS ITCH BABY IT'LL KEEP U HOWLIN TIL THE DAYLIGHT; (YES IT WILL) IT'LL KEEP U BURNIN ALL THRU THE NIGHT (IT WIIILLLL) IT'LL KEEP U HOWLIN TIL THE DAY LITE; IT'LL KEEP U CRYIN ALL THRU THE NITE VD WILL COME AND VD WILL GO; BUT HERPES

William E. "Tony" Franklin Jr

IS HERE TO STAY NOW DON'T U KNOW THAT IT'S GIVIN UP A PAIN SO BAD, THATS ONE PIECE OF PUSSY THAT U WISH U NEVA HAD chorus MUST BE THE HERPES (MUST BE THE HERPES) THAT'S BURNIN MY DICK; MUST BE THE HERPES (MUST BE THE HERPES) THAT MAKES MY BALLS ITCH MUST BE THE HERPEEES; NOW BABY THATS BURNIN MY DICK; MUST BE THE HERPES; THAT MAKES MY BALLS ITCH BABY IT'LL KEEP U HOWLIN TIL THE DAYLIGHT; (YES IT WILL) IT'LL KEEP U BURNIN ALL THRU THE NIGHT (IT WIIILLLL) IT'LL KEEP U HOWLIN TIL THE DAY LITE; IT'LL KEEP U CRYIN ALL THRU THE NITE RAP VD, GONORRHEA, AND THE CLAPS I ALL READY HAD, BUT HERPES CAN DO WHAT THEY ALL CAN DO AND EVEN TWICE AS BAD WHEN IT GOES TO WORK U'LL GO BERSERK CUZ IT HURTS WORSE IN EVERY WAY THE PUSSY WAS GOOD BUT U KNOW U SHOULDA USED A RUBBER ON A BITCH THAT DAY HI HO IT'S ON THE GO IT'LL KNOCK YOUR NUTTS RIGHT TO THE FLO WHEN YOU WANNA TRY TO GET UP AND GO IT'LL KNOCK YOU DOWN AGAIN

CUZ WE'RE TALKIN BOUT THE SHIT THEY CALL HERPE THE ONE THAT HURTS SO VISCIOUSLY AND IF U LOOK REAL CLOSE YOU'RE SURE TO FIND WHEN ITS DONE WITH YOUR DICK IT'LL GET IN YOUR BEHIND HEY HEY

Over the past several weeks I've been bombarded with emails and calls asking me if the stories in my Tirades are true. People seem to be amazed and somewhat skeptical when I tell them that the actual premise of my tales are historically accurate even if I take "liberties" with the "artistic interpretations" of some of them. The next question asked has been, "Was your Mama really like that?" My answer to that is; any story I tell about my mother/mothers sisters, brothers, cousins, aunts, uncles, grand parents, nieces, nephews, etc.; is COMPLETELY 100% WITHOUT ANY EMBELLISHMENTS, TRUE!

You see I am a product of the most mixed up family system you could possibly imagine. In my 46 years on this earth I've never met anyone who's "Family Structure" comes close to a comparison of mine. To this day I have not completely figured it out but I do know that right or wrong, good or bad; this "structure" has made me the person I am today AND given me these stories that you all seem to love, that I love telling; and the ability to convey them to you in an entertaining way. I have so enjoyed the 15 weeks of free therapy writing these has given me.

I thank you all for listening to my rants and raves and love you all for it

So today with a heavy heart I give you the last of "TONY'S TUESDAY TIRADES!!"

What better way to end this than to tell you all how it began. Here's my story;

ROOTS: THE MAKING OF THE TIRADER:

When I was born my mother, who had 5 kids before me, in a variety of different ways, was living with my father's sister (we'll call her A1 since she was the best) who had 8 kids of her own. Now my mama's other kids were parceled out all over the eastern seaboard. My oldest brother lived in Georgia with his aunt, 3 of my other siblings lived in North Carolina with what I believed to be a religious cult, and I had another sister who we didn't talk about because we didn't know if her daddy was my daddy, my older siblings daddy, "Uncle" Joes (Uncle Joe was the the NIGGA that coulda been the NC 3's daddy)or my mamas cousins husband (mama was a rolling stone. and quite fertile) who live somewhere around. One winter morning around 5am my 3 NC siblings were left on the steps of my aunts house (shoe and coatless). So my mama had to leave my aunts and find an apartment. when she did she took the 3 from NC. A1 (THANK GOD), made her leave me. So by the time i was 5, my aunt became my mother and her kids became my sisters and brothers. Are you with me so far?

A1's 2nd son had a son (we'll call him "BR" short for broken rubber) when i was 5. he lived w/us so growing up he became my baby brother, A1's 2nd daughter became attached to BR so he started calling her Mommy. Let me break it down for you; now my cousin/brother has a son who is my cousin/brother being raised by his sister who BR claims is his mama even though she's his aunt which makes her my cousin/sister/aunt I think.

When I was 6 My Birth mama had a son by my daddy (did I mention that my dad was married to an ugly ho in NY and my mama was married to so bamma here? that must've slipped my mind. SORRY) who went to live with my fathers other sister (we'll call her A2) who was dating my birth mama's daddy (he finally kicked heroin about 5 years prior). A2 decided she wanted to raise my brother as her own so my baby brother grew up thinking that, his mama was his sister, his granddaddy was his daddy, his brothers and sisters were his nieces and nephews. still with me? damn you all are very good because I lived this shit and I've been lost for years.

You all are probably saying "This shit can not be true" . I guess you're wondering how my mama's family got so screwed up. I'll tell you how;

WE HAD THE MOST FUCKED UP GRANDPARENTS YOU COULD POSSIBLY IMAGINE!!!! WE'RE LUCKY AS HELL THAT MY AUNTS AND UNCLES ONLY TURNED OUT TO ONLY DO SHIT THAT ABUSED THEMSELVES AND NOT BECOME THE FIRST BLACK SERIAL KILLER FAMILY! YOU DON'T BELIEVE ME? READ ON:

In the early 1950's my maternal grandparents and their 4 daughters and two sons moved from somewhere in the deep south to the DC area.

They were good God Fearing folks except for one minor character flaw that they both shared. They were casual heroin users. Now when they were in the backwoods of the Carolinas where the supply of their recreational drug was limited; it was not that big of a deal. BUT in the big city they found it prevalent which increased their usage and dependency. They began to lose themselves in the drug culture that took them by storm. Before long the drug life had consumed them and their family. Many a night you'd see the haunting silhouette of my infamous Nana (now referred to as "Grandma NOD" because of the way she stood. mama thought she had a spinal problem before she discovered her habit)) on the corner of 17th St with her mini-house dress and 6 inch orthopedic red pumps, with varicose veins that resembled old green fishnet stockings covering her legs. sellin a combination of pussy and ammonia (from the same source) with Grandpa "Dope" looking on from the front seat of his 1948 Car seat (that's all he had was the seat. He couldn't remember what kind of car it came from or if it actually came from a car). They had embraced the drug life and were out of control. Now, none of the children became users; but the addiction of their parents left them virtually parentless which led to most of them making choices they wouldn't have if they'd been properly supervised.

*I was the only 6 year old who hated his grand parents! Every time Grandpa dope came over the house he'd ask me "Let ya granddaddy hold a LIL somethin." And Grandma Nod would say "Baby, give your granny SNZZZZZZZZZZZZZZZZZZZZZZZZZZZZ, a dollar and I'll suck yo lil dick off! Make it 2 and I'll take my teef SNNNZZZZZZZZZZZ ZZZZZZZZZZZZZZZZZZZZZZZZZZZZZZ ZZZZZZZZZZZZZZZZZZZZZZZZZZZZZZ ZZZZZZZZZZZZZZZ (that's a NOD OFF! DON'T ACT LIKE YOU DON'T KNOW)out" Grandma took all my money!!!!!

Now with this family tree it's amazing how my generation of siblings has managed to not only survive but become vital members of society as well as loving nurturing parents, loyal friends, dedicated spouses, and most importantly brothers and sisters; even though we may not be biological, we are emotionally.

SO TO ALL MY BROTHERS/SISTERS/ COUSINS/NIECES/NEPHEWS/UNCLES/ AUNTS/MAMA/DADDYS; AND EVEN GRANDMA NOD AND GRANDPA DOPE;

<u>THANK YOU FOR BEING YOU AND MAKING ME</u>

<u>ME</u>

<u>FOR THE LAST TIME</u>

<u>I REALLY AM BETTER NOW</u>